ENGINEERING MARVELS
PYRAMIDS OF EGYPT

by Vanessa Black

pogo

Ideas for Parents and Teachers

Pogo Books let children practice reading informational text while introducing them to nonfiction features such as headings, labels, sidebars, maps, and diagrams, as well as a table of contents, glossary, and index.

Carefully leveled text with a strong photo match offers early fluent readers the support they need to succeed.

Before Reading

- "Walk" through the book and point out the various nonfiction features. Ask the student what purpose each feature serves.
- Look at the glossary together. Read and discuss the words.

Read the Book

- Have the child read the book independently.
- Invite him or her to list questions that arise from reading.

After Reading

- Discuss the child's questions. Talk about how he or she might find answers to those questions.
- Prompt the child to think more. Ask: What is the largest structure you have ever built? What was it made of? How long did it stand?

Pogo Books are published by Jump!
5357 Penn Avenue South
Minneapolis, MN 55419
www.jumplibrary.com

Library of Congress Cataloging-in-Publication Data

Names: Black, Vanessa, 1973- author.
Title: Pyramids of Egypt / by Vanessa Black.
Description: Minneapolis, MN: Jump!, Inc., 2017.
Series: Engineering marvels | Audience: Ages 7-10.
Includes bibliographical references and index.
Identifiers: LCCN 2017007367 (print)
LCCN 2017012557 (ebook) | ISBN 9781624965821
(e-book) ISBN 9781620317051 (hard cover: alk. paper)
Subjects: LCSH: Pyramids–Egypt–Juvenile literature.
Pyramids–Egypt–Design and construction–Juvenile
literature. | Building, Stone–Egypt–History–To 1500–
Juvenile literature. | Classification: LCC DT63 (ebook)
LCC DT63 .B545 2017 (print) | DDC 932–dc23
LC record available at https://lccn.loc.gov/2017007367

Editor: Kirsten Chang
Book Designer: Leah Sanders
Photo Researcher: Leah Sanders

Photo Credits: WitR/Shutterstock, cover; karimhesham/iStock, 1, 10; Orhan Cam/Shutterstock, 3; Joshua Dalsimer/Getty, 4; sculpies/iStock, 5; kasto80/iStock, 6-7; Dmitry Pichugin/Shutterstock, 8-9; Yann Arthus-Bertrand/Getty, 11; Grant Faint/Getty, 12-13; MU YEE TING/Shutterstock, 14-15; DragonImages/iStock, 16-17; Q-files.com, 16-17, 19; LUke1138/iStock, 18; AndreyPopov/iStock, 19; Peter de Clercq/Alamy, 20-21; Dmitry Melnikov/Shutterstock, 23.

Printed in the United States of America at Corporate Graphics in North Mankato, Minnesota.

TABLE OF CONTENTS

CHAPTER 1

STILL STANDING

Imagine you are on vacation in Egypt. Your family joins a tour group trekking across the sand. You get to ride a camel!

Three huge structures rise above the flat desert. What are they? The **Pyramids** of Giza!

The pyramids are near Cairo, Egypt. They are called Khufu, Khafre, and Menkaure. They were built more than 4,500 years ago. They have survived earthquakes, **looting**, and war. They are engineering marvels.

Khafre

Menkaure

Khufu

WHERE ARE THEY?

The Pyramids of Giza are near Cairo, Egypt.

TURKEY

Mediterranean Sea

LIBYA   **EGYPT**   Giza Cairo

■ = Pyramids of Giza

N
W ┼ E
S

The pyramids are **tombs** for **pharaohs**. Everything a king would need in the **afterlife** was buried with him. **Archaeologists** think that clothes, furniture, and even boats may have been in the tombs.

The biggest pyramid was for the king named Khufu. It is known as the Great Pyramid. It once stood about 480 feet (146 meters) high. That is taller than the Statue of Liberty! It was the world's tallest building for more than 4,000 years.

TAKE A LOOK!

What does it look like inside the Great Pyramid?

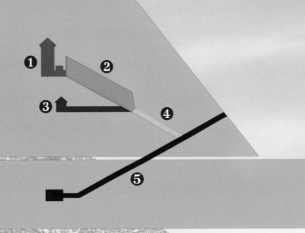

① **King's Chamber**
② **Grand Gallery**
③ **Queen's Chamber**
④ **Ascending Passage**
⑤ **Descending Passage**

CHAPTER 2

CONSTRUCTION

How did ancient Egyptians build such strong structures? It took skill. Every part of them was planned.

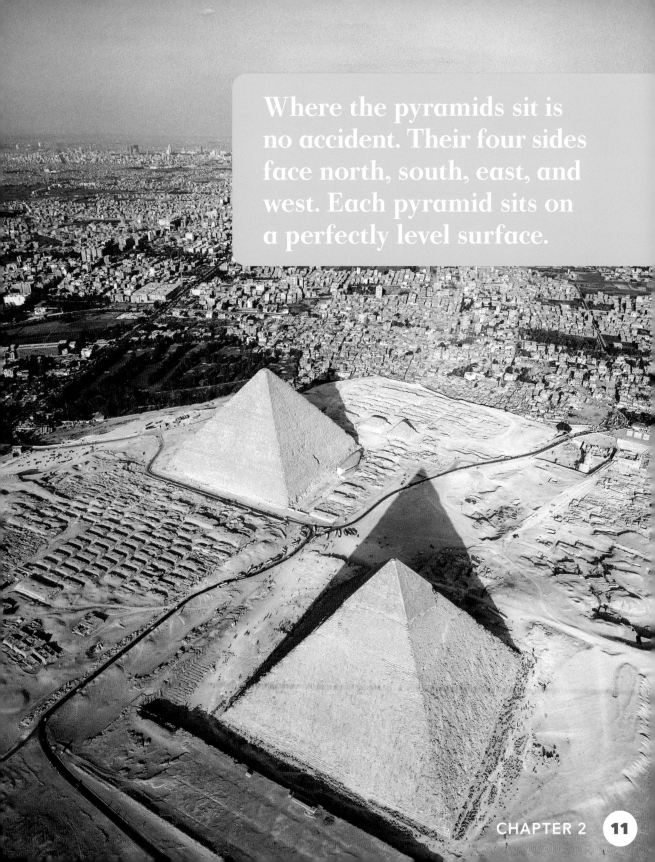

Where the pyramids sit is no accident. Their four sides face north, south, east, and west. Each pyramid sits on a perfectly level surface.

Archaeologists think the Egyptians used the stars to align the sides. They used **geometry** to measure angles.

DID YOU KNOW?

Workers used a plumb line to measure precisely. This tool has a small, heavy object tied to a string. It hangs straight down, making a vertical line.

It took about 20 years to build the Great Pyramid. It is made of about 2.3 million stone blocks. That is a lot of rock! Where did they get it? From all over Egypt.

DID YOU KNOW?

There are three small pyramids next to the Great Pyramid. They are sometimes called the queen's pyramids. They are part of the tomb for Khufu.

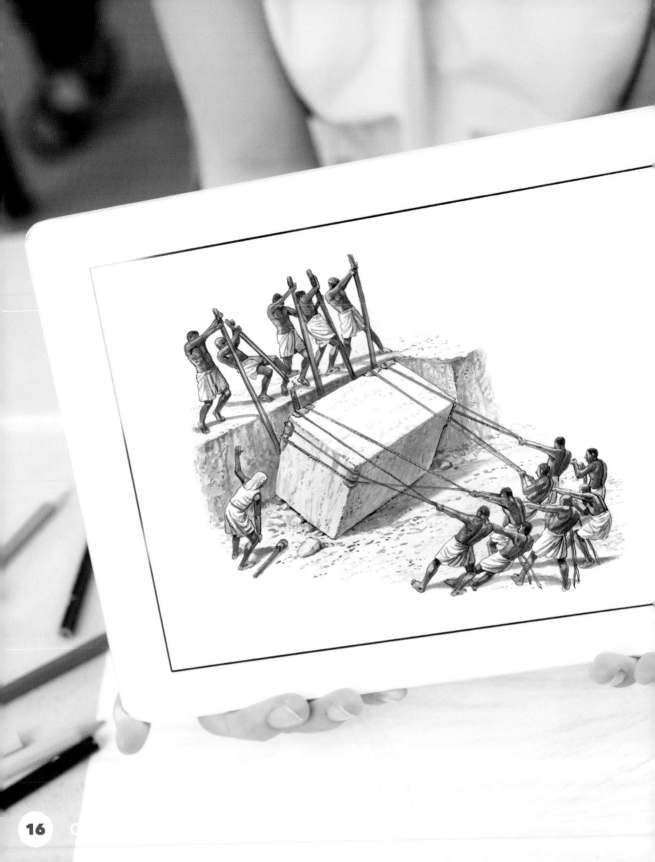

Quarries were set up. **Masons** cut the stones to exact sizes. They used hammers. They used chisels. Workers then moved the rocks to the job site. Some were moved by boat. Some were moved by sled.

DID YOU KNOW?

How did workers move the stones over the sand? By adding water to the sand! It is easier to pull sleds over wet sand.

CHAPTER 3

· ·

A MYSTERY

The stones were very heavy. Many weighed more than two tons (1.8 metric tons)! How did workers place them? No one knows for sure. There are many **theories**.

One is that they used ramps. When they were done, they took the ramps down. Another idea is that they used logs to roll the stones.

How the pyramids were built is a mystery. Archaeologists find new evidence all the time. Maybe one day we will solve the mystery of these marvels!

ACTIVITIES & TOOLS

BUILD A PYRAMID

Make a sweet recreation of the Great Pyramid in this activity.

What You Need:
- ruler
- sugar cubes
- tacky glue
- piece of cardboard

❶ Use the ruler to draw a square on the cardboard. This is the pyramid's base.

❷ Completely fill the base with sugar cubes, gluing as you go.

❸ Make the next layer, but move in one sugar cube all the way around.

❹ Make each layer until you make it to the top. The Great Pyramid of Giza was built this way, layer by layer. However, inside the Great Pyramid were passageways and rooms that were planned and built as each layer was laid. When built, workers placed white limestone for the last "casing" layer. This made the pyramid smooth (not stepped). It also made it gleam in the sunlight.

GLOSSARY

afterlife: The life that ancient Egyptians believed happened after death.

archaeologists: Scientists who study past human life and activities.

geometry: Math that has to do with points, lines, angles, surfaces, and solids.

looting: Stealing, sometimes destroying things in the process.

masons: Skilled workers that work with stones.

pharaohs: Ancient Egyptian kings.

pyramids: Structures with a square base and four triangular sides that meet at a point.

quarries: Places where a lot of rocks are cut from the ground.

theories: Ideas that are meant to explain facts.

tombs: Houses or burial chambers for dead people.

INDEX

TO LEARN MORE

Learning more is as easy as 1, 2, 3.

1) Go to www.factsurfer.com

2) Enter "PyramidsofEgypt" into the search box.

3) Click the "Surf" button to see a list of websites.

With factsurfer, finding more information is just a click away.